something after death?

something after death?

GEOFFREY PARRINDER

Argus Communications　　　　Niles, Illinois

ACKNOWLEDGEMENTS

Excerpt from *Memories, Dreams, Reflections* by C.G. Jung, translated by Richard and Clara Winston. Copyright © 1973 by Pantneon Books, a Division of Random House, Inc. Reprinted with permission.

Excerpt from *The Secret of the Golden Flower* by Richard Wilhelm. Copyright © 1970 by Harcourt Brace Jovanovich, Inc. Reprinted with permission.

PHOTO CREDITS

Doris Barker   7,11,29
Ron Church   49
John Dylong   25
Algirdas Grigaaitis   39,57
Jose L. Gonzalez/TOM STACK & ASSOCIATES   4
E. Hanumantha Rao/TOM STACK & ASSOCIATES   33
Thomas A. Henley/TOM STACK & ASSOCIATES   15,17
Brent Jones   23,63
Jean-Claude Lejeune   43
Bob McKendrick   53
Zanner Miller/TOM STACK & ASSOCIATES   59
Sue Moser   21

© Copyright Argus Communications 1975
7440 Natchez Avenue, Niles, Illinois 60648

Published in the U.S.A. under license from National Christian Education Council, Robert Denholm House, England.

© Geoffrey Parrinder 1974
All rights reserved. No part of this publication may be reproduced, stored in a retrieval system or transmitted in any form by any means—electronic, mechanical, photocopying, recording, or otherwise—without the prior permission of the copyright owner.

Printed in the United States of America
International Standard Book Number   0-913592-41-2
Library of Congress Number   75-18897

1   2   3   4   5   6   7   8   9   0

CONTENTS

Chapter 1 The Natural Way 5

2 Survival 8

3 The True Self 12

4 The Soul and God 19

5 Pre-existence and Rebirth 26

6 Memory 31

7 Experiences 36

8 Psychical Research 41

9 The Resurrection of Jesus 46

10 The Spiritual Body 51

11 Heaven 55

12 The Goals of Life 62

References 67

THE NATURAL WAY 1

"If a man dies, will he live again?" asked Job and was not sure of the answer.[1] There is one universal fact of life: we shall all die. This is the way of nature.

When we are young, most of us do not think about dying, because we are full of life, and growth is natural to us. "Threescore years and ten" is said to be the normal span of life, and nowadays many people live longer than that. Eighty, ninety, even a hundred years are now natural, with better health conditions, especially for women. But after the prime of life hair begins to go white or fall out, rheumatism often develops, and other ailments slow down the pace of life until death comes as the natural conclusion for a weakened body. When the will to live ceases, most people slip easily into death.

In many countries now, and in past ages, death might often come earlier, from sudden disease or warfare. In the eighteenth century a Scottish thinker said that life is "nasty, brutish, and short." Even in our more comfortable surroundings, there may come a tragedy, the suffering of somebody we know well or love, and we realize that life is not all easy or guaranteed to be long for everyone. Then we ask: "Why does this happen? Why does it happen to me, or to my friend?" And behind this question is the feeling that suffering and early death are unnatural.

Most of us in the Western world are cushioned against the tragedies of life, unless we are so unfortunate as to live during a war when destruction rains from the skies. But in a time of peace, and in a welfare state, death is usually far away from youth, and if it comes in ripe old age it is easier to understand. After all, we cannot continue to live forever, because the earth would not support such a greatly increased population. Bernard Shaw, in his play *Back to Methuselah,* imagined a world in which disease had been abolished and people lived for centuries until they had their "accident," by falling down or being run over. But such long lives are not likely, at least in our time, and it is curious that the notion of living for centuries seems undesirable, and again unnatural. It would bring more problems than it would solve.

It is to be expected that old people should think more about dying, for they are nearer to it. Old age brings many problems, and those who have no friends are lonely and afraid of the future. But those who are healthy and well cared for also wonder about the future. Their bodies are weaker than in youth, but their minds may be alert and even better developed than before. If they have a religious faith, they may talk about going to heaven or joining their loved ones who have gone before. Even without faith it is difficult for any of us to think that his spirit will be snuffed out. We all have a sense of our self, which seems to be more than the body, and it is hard to think that this will die.

In days gone by, when life was shorter and more diseases were fatal, perhaps people thought more about death. Today old people are often put in hospitals or homes, diseases and accidents are rushed out of sight, funeral ceremonies are cut to the minimum, and cremation removes the need to care for graves. Perhaps we suffer from a "fear of death," of anything unpleasant or awkward, until we are brought face to face with reality in our own suffering or other people's. Then we discover not only the fact of death, but the age-old question: "Is death the end?"

Shakespeare expressed this question in Hamlet's speech:

> To die, to sleep;
> To sleep! perchance to dream: ay, there's the rub;
> For in that sleep of death what dreams may come,
> When we have shuffled off this mortal coil,
> Must give us pause.[2]

If a man dies, will he live again?

SURVIVAL 2

In practically every country and every age there has been a belief that death is not the end, that something survives the destruction of man's physical body. This is perhaps the oldest religious belief of mankind, and there is evidence that it existed in many forms.

In ancient caves near Peking in China, and in various stone-age sites in Europe, there are graves or remains at least 100,000 years old which show that skulls were believed to contain vital powers which could be passed from one person to another. Bones were painted red to give them life in the hereafter. Men were buried with axes beside them, or women with cooking pots, which it was thought they would use in the life after death. The dead were buried with knees drawn up, like unborn babies, suggesting the hope of another birth. Paintings in caves suggest the influence of spiritual powers over animals. Finally, it is reasonable to assume that some of the most primitive men who survive today have certain beliefs like those of prehistoric men, and there is no human group, however primitive, which lacks an idea of a spiritual life, a life which is more than the body and survives death.

Is this belief in survival of death wishful thinking? Do men seem unable to envisage their own annihilation? It may be so, and the fact that men want to survive does not prove that they do so. But this belief has been held at all stages of human development, and not only by ignorant or shallow people. Survival has been argued by learned men all down the ages, and they have given many other reasons for this belief which we shall consider.

Socrates was condemned to death in Athens for atheism in the fourth century B.C. The charge was not true, except that Socrates had criticized some of the immoral stories of the deeds of the old Greek gods, and he sought for the truth which would be above the traditional laws of society. In his speech in defense of his life, Socrates considered whether death is the end or not:

> The state of death is one of two things:
> either the dead man wholly ceases to be,
> and loses all sensation; or, according to
> the common belief, it is a change and
> a migration of the soul to another place. . . .
> But now the time has come, and we must go hence;
> I to die, and you to live. Whether life or
> death is better is known to God, and to God only.[3]

Socrates was condemned to die by taking hemlock poison, and a final scene was described in which he was lying down calmly while his sorrowing friends gathered round. His last word was to ask a friend to offer a cock to Asclepius, the god of healing. This is taken to refer to the offering usually made in thanks for recovery from illness, for death is a recovery from the fever of life.[4]

Many arguments can be given for belief in survival of death, and these will be discussed later. Basic to most of them is a conviction that the human being is more than his body and that this "more" is not limited by space or time.

Certainly something survives death, for there is change and recreation. Every autumn brings decay, with death shown in beautiful colors; every spring brings new life. There is a cycle of life, going round and round, from life to death and back to life again. Job saw this, and looked beyond it:

> There is hope for a tree
> if it is cut down,
> that it will sprout again. . . .
> But man dies and wastes away;

> Yes, man gives up the spirit,
> and where is he? [5]

Trees and plants are renewed, but animal bodies decay and die. Yet they do not become nothing; they gradually change into something else. If men live in a hot dry country they see the dead soon becoming dust, and they say, "ashes to ashes, dust to dust." If the body is embalmed, it may last for centuries or millennia, and the British Museum has preserved bodies that are 6,000 years old, still with hair, teeth and skin. But whether decay comes quickly or slowly, nothing is totally destroyed. Scientists tell us that matter is indestructible; it may change its form, but new forms appear in due course. Our bodies do not become nothing; even if they are cremated, they take a different form in the universal whole.

From prehistoric times men have been convinced that they are more than bodies. Primitive men knew that the bodies they buried had been killed or died of disease. They realized that the weapons or cooking pots placed by corpses could not be used by those inert bodies, but they believed that some essence of the dead person could use the essence of the weapon and live a new life in the happy hunting grounds, or the Elysian Fields where the Greeks thought the dead continued their earthly occupations. Men have changed their ideas about the nature of life after death. But that something survives which is the true essence of a person has been held throughout the history of the world, and this is the theme of our next chapter.

> In practically every country
> and every age
> there has been a belief
> that death is not the end,
> that something survives
> the destruction on man's physical body.

THE TRUE SELF 3

We are all different people. We have different faces, thank goodness, for it would be very dull if everybody looked the same. We have separate identities, and we have individual minds. The world is not a great machine, for there are millions of living, thinking beings in it.

As we walk down a crowded street, we see countless other people, each with his own thoughts and hopes and fears. They go in different directions, and while they pay some attention to the traffic and the shops, these people also have an inner life going on in their minds. They are rather like sleepwalkers. Some of them are thinking about their homes, others about boy or girl friends, others about holidays or money or power. Many of us have fantasies about what we would do if we were airplane pilots or clever surgeons, and we wake up with a shock by bumping into somebody else.

Thomas Carlyle once pictured a man looking down from a tower and asking where the people came from:

> That living flood, pouring through these streets,
> of all qualities and ages,
> knowest thou whence it is coming,
> whither it is going? . . .
> From Eternity, onwards to Eternity!
> These are Apparitions: what else?
> Are they not Souls rendered visible:
> in Bodies, that took shape and will lose it,
> melting into air?

> Their solid Pavement is a Picture of the Sense;
> they walk on the bosom of Nothing,
> blank Time is behind them and before them.[6]

This is a poetical exaggeration, because the pavement is solid enough if we fall down on it. What is meant is that people not only live in a dream world, but they are souls which come from an unknown past and go to an unknown future.

We all have an inner life, which is very complex. We have dreams and fantasies about the future; we also have memories of the past. We have impulses which urge us to ideals of success or service to others or which tempt us to greed and possessiveness. We have our own thoughts and abilities to learn from others. There is an ego or center of self-interest which may be concerned largely with our own gains. But many teachers have said that there is something in us which is beyond the ego and self-interest.

When we talk about ourselves, we assume that we are not just bodies. My true "self" is what I cannot see in a mirror and can never observe as other people observe it. My body may be tall or short, fat or thin, but it is not my innermost self. That is related to my body but not identical with it.

In India thinkers for many centuries have discussed the nature of man and his true self or soul. They came to believe that this self is eternal, never born and never dying, and that it is the vital principle in the body. In the Upanishads, "secret sessions" in the form of talks by teachers and hearers, the self is described as dwelling in the body, like a king in a city with nine gates. The gates are the openings of the body: eyes, ears, nostrils, mouth, and lower organs; through these gates the soul acts on the world outside. In its actions it flutters like a great bird, but really it controls all the world—the activities of all beings.

> Embodied in a city with nine gates
> the soul flutters backwards and forwards
> like a great bird.
> It controls the whole world,
> both what is moving and what is unmoving.[7]

The innermost self is not just a part of the body. It is rather the principle that gives life and thought to the body. It is not the brain, for that perishes when the body dies. The Indian teachers discussed these problems at great length. The Buddha, who founded one of the world's greatest religions, thought that the soul could not be located or fully understood, but he made a clear distinction between the soul or self and the physical body.

> The body is not the soul,
> because if it was the soul
> the body could not become sick,
> and it would be possible to say
> "Let my body be like this or not like that."
> But the body can become ill
> just because it is not the soul.[8]

The argument continues by saying that feelings are not the soul, and consciousness is not the soul. These elements of the body can all be located, and they will all dissolve at death. We cannot point to any visible part of the body as permanent, but freedom from the passions and troubles of life will come when we get beyond bodily things to the calm of eternity. The Buddha thought that the nature of the soul cannot be described, but he taught that there is something which is uncreated and eternal, a being or state which is beyond all change and death.

Chinese thinkers too thought that there is an innermost self which is the reality beyond all change. One famous writing calls this the splendor which dwells in the square inch beyond the face and compares it to a place within a house within a field.

> In the field of the square inch
> of the house of the square foot,
> life can be regulated.

> *People not only live in a dream world,*
> *but they are souls*
> *which come from an unknown past*
> *and go to an unknown future.*

> The house of the square foot is the face.
> The field of the square inch in the face.
> could be no other than the Heavenly Heart.
> In the middle of the square inch dwells the splendor.[9]

This inner self is compared to the center of life, the dwelling place of light, the master within.

In Christian teaching the kingdom of God is to come on earth, but it is also within us. The pearl of great price, the seed growing in secret, the treasure hidden in a field, are pictures of the kingdom of God, but they have often been interpreted as the true self of man, precious beyond all wealth. So it does not profit a man anything, if he gains the whole world and loses his soul.

In modern times there is a great emphasis on the importance of the wholeness of personality. If we are developed in a one-sided way, exclusively physical or exclusively mental, then we are unbalanced. Many people are mentally ill because their personalities are divided or part of them is starved or distorted. Healing and wholeness go together, and this means not only healthy bodies but healthy minds, with every part of the self given full scope. Instead of seeking selfish gains, we need to get to the deeper center of our being, our whole self, which is joined to our body and beyond it and which is eternal.

Human beings are more than animals. We do not know a great deal about the consciousness of animals, but it seems that they do not reflect on their past or plan for the future. They seem to have little or no self-consciousness, knowledge of themselves as individuals, and they do not know that they will die.

Man is much weaker in body than some animals, but he can conquer them by his thought. The mathematician Pascal said:

> Man is only a reed,
> the weakest thing in nature,
> but he is a reed that thinks.[10]

*My true "self"
is what I cannot see in a mirror
and can never observe
as other people observe it.*

Human beings have a consciousness of themselves. They know that their bodies will die, but all the great religious teachers have been sure that death will not kill our real selves. Jesus said:

> Do not be afraid of those who can kill the body,
> but after that have no more that they can do.[11]

It is God alone who has power over both soul and body, and the need for belief in God arises largely out of man's belief in his immortal soul, and we shall now turn to this subject.

THE SOUL AND GOD 4

The millions of people in the world are visible facts, but where do they come from? Are they just the product of nature, of blind evolution? If so, how is it they too are not blind? How can living beings have minds which are greater than the unthinking nature which produced them?

The ancient Indians meditated for centuries on these problems. There is a passage in the Upanishads which asks the questions that men have asked over and over again in the past and are still asking today:

> Where do we come from?
> How do we live? What supports us?
> Is it Time that was the cause?
> Or was it Nature, or Necessity, or Chance,
> or the Elements, or some Person?
> Or was it all these together?
> No, it cannot be so, because of the existence of
> the Soul.

But having dismissed blind Nature or Fate or Accident, this teacher is forced to conclude that there must be a God whose power has created and moved everything.

> Some wise men talk about the power of Nature,
> and others speak about Time.
> They are deluded!
> Because it is the power of God
> in the world that sets all things going.[12]

If human beings are intelligent, there must have been an intelligent Creator to produce them. In another chapter in the Upanishads a father is talking to his son about the impossibility of life and thought coming out of what is lifeless and unthinking. Some people have thought that way, but it is ridiculous and illogical.

> To be sure there are some people who say
> that in the beginning the world was just
> nonexistence, a blank holding together,
> and that from such nonexistence
> living Being was produced.
> But really, how could that happen?
> How could existence come out of nonexistence?
> No, on the contrary.
> In the beginning this world was undivided Being.[13]

In most religions there are texts which speak of the creation of the world or the existence of universal and conscious Being. Creation comes either by acts of God, or from a conscious Power which in China was called the Way (Tao). About the third century B.C. a Chinese writer composed, "The Way and its Power" (Tao Te Ching), which has been a very popular and influential work ever since. This constantly speaks of the power of the Way.

> There was something which existed
> before heaven and earth;
> it had no form and yet it was complete.
> It was mysterious, silent and changeless.
> It may be called the Mother of all things. . . .
> The Way gave birth to the One,
> then to two and three,
> up to the thousands of things in the world.[14]

But whether it is called the Way, or Being, or a creator, it is its relationship to the soul of man that is important for us. If we are

> *It is because of his inner being,*
> *his spiritual self,*
> *that man has come*
> *to awareness of God.*

to get further in understanding survival of death, we must explore the relationship of the soul, the true self or essence of man, with God or the Supreme Self. It is because of his inner being, his spiritual self, that man has come to an awareness of God. The teacher whom we quoted from the Indian Upanishads speaks of his soul as small and invisible and also greater than nature. Finally it merges into the divine Being.

> This Soul within my heart is smaller
> than a grain of rice or barley or mustard
> or millet, or a kernel of millet.
> This Soul within my heart is greater
> than the earth, the air, the sky
> and all the worlds. . .
> This is my Soul within my heart,
> this is the All
> and when I die I shall merge into it.[15]

The soul is spiritual, a nonmaterial essence, and at death it will return to the All, the power from which it came. Or it might be said that mind, the human mind, will return to the divine Mind from which it emerged.

If the soul of man is going somewhere after death, it must have come from somewhere. In the Bible it is said that man came from the breath or spirit of God, and this must be immortal.

> The Lord God formed man
> of the dust of the ground,
> and breathed into his nostrils
> the breath of life,
> and man became a living soul.[16]

Then at the end of life the spirit which had been breathed into man goes back to the creator.

*God acts to save those
who think about him
and love him.*

> The dust returns to the earth as it was
> and the spirit returns to God who gave it.[17]

Not only have men believed in a God who is greater than themselves, their creator and final destiny, but they have also believed that God cares for them. So God will save men who trust in him, in this life and after death as well. The most famous Indian poem and scripture, the Bhagavad Gita, composed about the third century B.C., says that God acts to save those who think about him and love him.

> Those who meditate on me and worship me,
> with their thoughts enter into me,
> then quickly I become their Savior
> from the sea of the round of deaths.[18]

In the Bible Paul declares that nothing in heaven or earth, in life or death, could separate us from the love of God.

> I am certain that neither life nor death . . .
> nor things present nor things to come . . .
> nor height nor depth nor any other creature
> will be able to separate us from the love of
> God.[19]

A conviction that death cannot be the end comes in all religions, and it finds further emphasis in those religions which believe that God loves man and will never let him go, in this life or the next. Not only the notion that there is a God, but that God is love, brings the hope of eternal life through his power and goodness. The knowledge of God gives eternal life: "this is eternal life that they should know you as the only true God."[20] But "God so loved" the world that he sent salvation for everyone:

> that whoever believes in him
> should not perish
> but have eternal life.[21]

Is death the end?

PRE-EXISTENCE
AND REBIRTH 5

If the soul is immortal, it will not only continue to exist after death, but it also must have lived before birth on earth. So we ask not only, is there something after death? but, is birth the beginning?—not only postexistence but preexistence. This arises from the very nature of the soul, which is an eternal essence. As it cannot die, so it cannot be born out of nothing. In the Bhagavad Gita we read:

> The soul is not born, and it never dies.
> It did not come into existence,
> and it will never cease to exist.
> It is unborn, eternal, primal, everlasting.[22]

The belief in preexistence has been especially strong in India, spreading from there to China and eastern Asia. It has not been discussed much in the West, though it might be taken to be implied in the Bible verse which says that God breathed into man his spirit, for the spirit of God must be immortal and eternal. But popular European belief, when it has been concerned with the matter at all, has usually been based on the assumption that the soul was created at birth or at conception, and it has not developed the notion of many previous lives of the same soul.

Yet some of our poets write about preexistence. Perhaps some of us have had an experience similar to that of Dante Gabriel Rossetti:

> I have been here before,
> But when or how I cannot tell;

> I know the grass beyond the door
> The sweet keen smell,
> The sighing sound, the lights around the shore.
> I knew it all of yore.

And Wordsworth wrote:

> Our birth is but a sleep and a forgetting:
> The Soul that rises with us, our life's star,
>   Hath had elsewhere its setting,
>   And cometh from afar:
>   Not in entire forgetfulness,
>   And not in utter nakedness,
> But trailing clouds of glory do we come
>   From God, who is our home.[23]

But even when Wordsworth wrote about the preexistence of the soul, and its forgetfulness at birth, he considered it to have come from God and not from other lives on earth.

Some of the ancient Greeks wondered about the possibility of previous births. Plato considered that men must have lived on earth before, because they have inborn ideas of goodness and beauty which must have been acquired in another life. Plato said that

> There is ancient belief, which we remember,
> that on leaving this world the souls of men
> exist in the next world, and that they return here
> and are born again from the dead.
> But if it is true that the living are born
> from the dead, our souls must exist in the other
> world, otherwise they could not be born again. . . .
> If, as we are forever repeating, beauty and good,
> and the other ideas really exist . . .
> then, just as they exist, our souls must have
> existed before ever we were born.[24]

In a story at the end of his great book on the ideal state, *The Republic,* Plato talks about a man called Er who seemed to have been killed in battle. But after twelve days, as his body was being prepared for the funeral, Er came to life again and described what he had seen in the other world. His soul had traveled with others who had been killed on the battlefield, until they came to two gaps in earth and heaven, where judges were sitting and commanding the just people to take the road to heaven and the unjust to go down into the earth. Er himself was told to watch and take a report back home later. Then he saw two other gaps by which souls came back up from the earth or down from heaven, the just talking about the happiness they had received, and the unjust telling of all their sufferings.

All the souls then proceeded to a new place where they drew lots to choose their destiny in the next life on earth. They would choose power, beauty, skill, high birth, and so on, combined with disease, poverty, or short life. Many people chose badly, including some who came from heaven, but had never known the discipline of trouble and so were careless. Some others who came up from earth chose more wisely because they had suffered affliction. Then all of them were sent through the Plain of Forgetfulness and drank of its river, so that they would not recall their previous lives. Er himself did not drink and was strangely preserved, awaking at dawn with the memory of the past and the future that he could give others.[25]

Plato's story is similar to the first statement of belief in rebirth which is found in the Upanishads and which has influenced much of Asia ever since. Here a young man went to a meeting of rulers, who asked if his father, a priest, had instructed him properly. When he said yes, they asked,

> Do you know where people go after death?
> Do you know how they come back again?
> Do you know why heaven is not full
> with people always dying?[26]

The boy could not answer any of these questions and went back to complain to his father, who had to admit his own ignorance. The priestly father then went to the rulers and asked for instruction, which they said had formerly been known only to the rulers.

At death, they told him, those who had knowledge and self-denial when they were cremated would pass through the flame to the highest spiritual worlds and would never come back to be reborn on earth. But those who kept to rituals and activities would pass into the cremation smoke and come back again. However, there was a further choice, for those whose actions had been good would return to a good life in the best families, but those whose deeds had been evil would have evil births in the lowest human or animal families.

This Indian statement about the rebirth of souls on earth from a previous earthly life is like Plato's story, and similarly it has a strong moral element. Men are not just born again naturally, but their state in life is decided by the kind of life they had lived before. In India this was called Karma, meaning "deeds" and the results of deeds.

> According to one's deeds, so does one become;
> the doer of good becomes good,
> the doer of evil becomes evil.[27]

If such a theory of Karma and rebirth is accepted, it provides an explanation for the different states of people on earth, for their joys and sorrows. If a man is born a cripple or in great poverty, then it is blamed on his own actions in a previous life. This may seem quite unproved and of no comfort to the sick or poor person, but is not thought to be unfair because it is following a principle of justice from the past.

Karma is a kind of fate, following the actions supposed to have been committed in past lives. But it is not an unchangeable fate for the future. Indeed everybody is supposed to try to improve his lot on earth or live a patient and helpful life, and then in the next life his destiny will improve. Those who do not accept the ideas of Karma and reincarnation will question the truth of these conclusions, but to hundreds of millions of Hindus, Buddhists, and others right across Asia, these are facts of life which explain its present inequalities and encourage men to work for a better future.

MEMORY 6

Rebirth into several, perhaps thousands, of lives is taken for granted in most of Asia, and it follows from the principle of the eternal nature of the soul. Changing from one life to another is like putting on a new suit of clothes: the outside changes, but the inner person remains the same.

> When his clothes wear out, a man puts them away
> and takes new and different ones,
> and so the embodied soul will put away
> the worn out bodies and take new and other ones.[28]

This is the basic teaching of the famous Bhagavad Gita. The warrior Arjuna is troubled at the sight of the coming battle against his relatives and friends, and he refuses to fight. But his charioteer, the God Krishna, assures him that even if their bodies are killed, his own and those of his enemies, yet all their souls are imperishable.

> These bodies come to an end . . .
> but the soul is not born and it never dies.[29]

None of these Indian books which have been quoted refers to memory—why we do not remember our previous lives. If I have lived before, I ought to be able to remember it. If I cannot remember the good or evil of a past life, what is the value of those experiences to me?

Several answers have been given to this problem. Plato thought that men drink of a river of forgetfulness before birth and cannot remember either their previous lives or heaven and hell. The character of the soul, he thought, is shaped by the changing circumstances of life, and it is this character that is important rather than knowledge of details of the past.

Many things of which we have no recollection have happened to us during our earthly life, for our memory is highly selective and it picks some things to recall out of multitudes of past experiences. In dreams we see many pictures, most of which we never recall, and in dreamless sleep we pass beyond all recall; yet when we awake, we have a conviction of the continuity of our own self without any break. Similarly there seems no reason why we could not have the same feeling of our own self as we have now, in some future life, even if then we have no memory of this present life.

The eternal soul does not depend upon past history, though nearly all theories of a future life hold that the past affects the future, even when there is no recollection of the past.

It is remarkable that the classical Hindu texts do not claim memories of the past as proof of a previous existence. Their argument is based on the nature of the soul as undying and unborn because it is indestructible. So whether we can remember a past life or not is unimportant; the vital matter is the eternity of the soul, which passes through many lives like a rider in a chariot.

When I see a business director being driven through a city by a chauffeur in an executive car and unconcerned about the traffic while he reads over the papers for his next board meeting, I think of the soul in its chariot. Its outer shell experiences the changes of life, but its inmost essence remains untouched by them.

*Changing
from one life to another
is like putting on
a new suit of clothes:
the outside changes,
but the inner person
remains the same.*

Some later texts do discuss memories of the past and visions of the future which come to a fully enlightened man, who has all knowledge and wisdom. These appear in popular stories of the Buddha.

These indicate a continuity between various stages of life and relate that the Buddha himself, at his enlightenment, remembered all his own past lives.

> I turned my mind to recall its former dwellings,
> and I remembered their variety,
> from one birth to a hundred or a thousand. . . . .
> I was born to a certain family,
> with a certain name and a certain color,
> and was fed, and had pleasant and painful states
> until the end of that life span.[30]

A very popular collection of Buddhist narratives, the Birth Stories (Jatakas), contains some 550 tales about previous births of the Buddha, as merchant, king, young man, fairy, animal and others. And at the end of many of these stories the Buddha declares, "I myself was that merchant," "that king," "that young man," "that fairy," "that animal."

In popular belief countless Hindus and Buddhists and other Asians believe not only that they have lived on earth before but that they remember their past lives. Stories are told of husband and wife who spend the next life looking for each other, if they were deeply in love, or avoiding each other if they were not. Fortune tellers claim to be able to predict the future from memories of past lives, and accidents and marvels are supposed to prove the power of the past over the present.

Yet the belief in rebirth depends on the immortality of the soul, which can go from one habitation to another. The Buddha, though he remembered his past lives when he had gained perfect knowledge, also saw beings dying and being born at present according to the quality of their Karma, and he finally saw the way out of the cycle of rebirth. Release would come by understanding the power of desire and breaking its hold upon the mind by mental and spiritual discipline.

The cycle of rebirth is a great chain, of birth, and death, and rebirth, and redeath. It goes on through thousands of lives for most people, until men cry out for salvation, "Oh save me, I am like a frog in a waterless well."

Not only souls but the whole universe is gripped in a cycle of change. There is creation, then maturity, and finally dissolution. So some Hindu gods have three faces or heads, showing their characters as creators, sustainers, and destroyers. Destruction with pain and suffering is part of life, and souls revolve in inner circles like the universe in a vast outer circle. But destruction is not the end, for dissolution gives way in time to recreation, re-emergence of the round of life. In pictorial form, the universe emerges from the body of God, flourishes for a time, and then is absorbed again in the divine body until the next emergence. Some teachers spoke of the souls as parts of the body of God, though they were not identical with him because the individual parts are much smaller than the whole.

Belief in immortal souls and their rebirth does not necessarily involve belief in God. Reincarnation could be a natural process like evolution, or perhaps more like a theory in physics which speaks of a "steady state" of the universe, but belief in God or some divine being does appear very often, especially when life seems unjust or when it seems impossible for man to save himself by his own efforts. While Asians believe that they are caught up in the round of births and conditioned by their own past Karma, they want to get out of this iron cycle.

Three ways are taught for liberation or salvation from the round of births. Perfect knowledge can bring release into passionless Nirvana, but this way is hard and few people find it. Works, accumulating good Karma, may bring liberation in time, but it is a long path, through many births. So, love of God is widely claimed as the quickest and best way, for the grace of God lifts man out of the round of births and deaths.

In the end we face the same question, after one life or many: What is the lot of the soul in its final destination? What is the goal of life? What is Heaven or Nirvana? But before we come to these problems, we must consider some other important claims to produce evidence for survival after death.

EXPERIENCES 7

Argument alone rarely convinces people, but experiences arouse emotions which may bring conviction. Can we claim an experience of a *future* life? Hardly, for ourselves, but perhaps we may have an experience of somebody who has lived before, or someone else may claim to have had such an experience.

As I write this, a West Indian friend has been staying in my home. On her first night here she thought she heard noises downstairs and thought about the cockroaches which get into food in the tropics. She went downstairs but saw everything was put away and remembered that there are no cockroaches here. She was returning upstairs when she saw Katie. Katie died ten years ago, and my friend had only seen her once before. But Katie was one of my oldest friends, had lived in my house, and had died in the hospital not long after she left here.

I did not have this experience, and I have never seen a ghost, so I asked for details. What was Katie wearing? The dress she had on when my friend saw her the first time. Did she speak? No, she was standing by my mother's room, who had been her close companion for thirty years. Was this appearance a projection from my friend's mind? She is "psychic" and has had many such experiences. But can I say that she is mistaken? What is a projection anyway? Does it mean that there is nothing there? Or that something has been sent out from my friend's mind? And what is that? Can it have no relationship with Katie or with anyone else?

Was this experience imagination, and what is imagination? In Bernard Shaw's play, *Saint Joan,* Joan of Arc declared that she heard voices from God and his angels. Her critics told her that the voices came from her imagination, and Joan retorted,

> Of course,
> that is how the messages
> of God come to us.[31]

Many of us may not have had any kind of feeling or sight of the presence of somebody we knew well who has died, and we may deny that "ghosts" exist or be afraid of seeing them. But it is likely that many more people have had some kind of experience of the presence of their departed friends than would admit it easily. In many countries people certainly do claim to have some contacts with the departed. In our artificial civilization, where we live in crowded and noisy cities, with television preventing us from thinking for ourselves, we may be blind and deaf to spiritual influences.

There is a popular hymn that has these lines:

> Time, like an ever-rolling stream,
> Bears all its sons away.

But the next two lines are clearly untrue,

> They fly forgotten, as a dream
> Dies at the opening day.[32]

Many of those who have died in past ages are not forgotten; "Their name lives for evermore." All the founders of great religions, many heroes and thinkers of history, are still remembered, some after thousands of years. Ordinary people are also remembered, often by name and in detail, in the services and prayers for the dead which are practiced in many religions, and which we may neglect today with that "fear of death" which is modern but unnatural.

In China, though not only there, "ancestor worship," or veneration of the dead, was a central part of traditional religion, and it was so described thirty years ago:

There is a family shrine in every household, rich or poor. It is usually situated in that part of the house that faces west. It is always in the middle room of the second floor, on a specially built wooden platform. The name of each ancestor is written on a wooden tablet, together with his or her age at death. . . . These tables are either housed in single wooden pavilions or in double husband-wife pavilions. The tablets of dear ones are often decorated with colored silk. These tablets are arranged in order. In front of them are always offerings of dishes of food, incense tripods, candlesticks, and a vase of fresh or artificial flowers.[33]

In the last thirty years many things have changed in China. The cult of the emperor has been replaced by the cult of Chairman Mao, who is declared to be the ever-living red sun which will never die. His words in the *Little Red Book* are learned by heart and treasured like the Bible or the Koran. Many of the old gods and teachings are gone, but they have been replaced by new heroes and new dogmas. Yet people keep on dying, and old people still give offerings and remember the names of those whose company they will soon join, and it is likely that this will long remain.

After listing many of the unforgotten heroes of faith, the Bible speaks of us as "surrounded by a great cloud of witnesses."[34] Many ordinary people often have a feeling of the nearness of their close relatives and friends who have "passed away."

I myself have often felt the closeness of my father, my wife's parents, and other dear, departed friends.

Many churches and other religions have services with special prayers for the dead. There are invocations of the saints, services

In spirit
we each other greet,
And shall again
each other see.

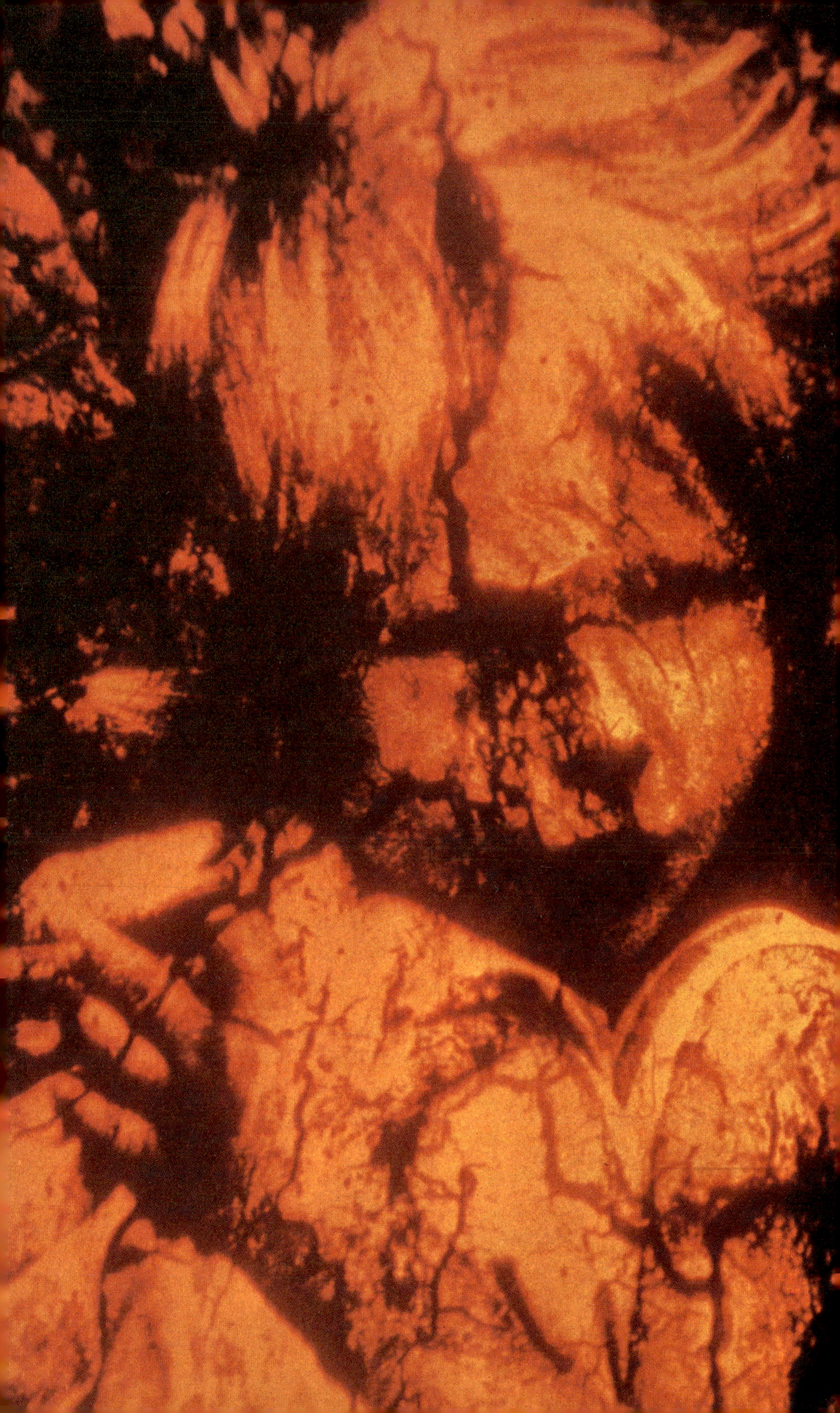

not only at burials but daily prayers for the dead "in memoriam" services at anniversaries, and commemorations of all the faithful departed, "All Saints" for special heroes of faith, and "All Souls" for every other believer. In the Apostles' Creed the words, "I believe in . . . the Communion of Saints" is usually taken to mean the fellowship of those who have passed over with their friends who are still on earth.

Richard Baxter, a seventeenth-century Puritan writer, wrote about this communion of saints which brings an assurance of the future and a daily meeting in prayer:

> As for my friends, they are not lost;
>   The several vessels of thy fleet,
> Thought parted now, by tempests tossed,
>   Shall safely in the heaven meet. . . .
>
> Before thy throne we daily meet,
>   As joint petitioners to thee;
> In spirit we each other greet,
>   And shall again each other see.

PSYCHICAL RESEARCH 8

In addition to the innumerable experiences of ordinary people thinking about their departed friends, many special claims have been made of sights of or voices from the dead, such as my friend's sight of Katie. Some would be claimed as simple visions, while others would be called regular "ghosts," who have appeared to different people over long periods, and "hauntings" would be claimed for them.

It is very difficult to test such claims and to distinguish between "genuine" and "imagination" or simple fraud. For nearly a hundred years the Society for Psychic Research has investigated such matters. This means not only the study of the soul (*psyche*) but examination of conditions which appear to be beyond the general scope of physical laws and may have been caused by spiritual forces. Psychic research has tried to examine reports of ghosts, apparitions, clairvoyance, haunted houses, spiritualistic seances, and so on.

There are people, like my friend, who may be called "psychic," meaning that they believe they are sensitive to invisible influences, but they would not normally try to obtain regular communications from the dead. Then there are organized meetings of people like the Spiritualists, who hold regular or formal seances. A seance is a "session," in which one person, usually a woman, acts as "medium," that is, an intermediary between the living and the dead. She goes into a trance, and it is claimed that words which she then speaks are not her own but come from some other power or dead person. There may also be physical manifestations. Hands or faces may appear, so it is

41

claimed, though these are some of the most criticized aspects of spiritualistic practice.

One of the most famous spiritualists in literature was the medium of En-dor in the Bible. She used to be called "the witch of En-dor," but this was a mistake since the word "witch" does not occur in the text but only at the top of the page in old translations. The woman is called one who had "a familiar spirit," and she was clearly a medium who was believed to communicate with the dead. King Saul went in disguise to consult her before a fatal battle and asked her to call up the dead prophet Samuel who had been his advisor. The woman apparently went into a trance and described Samuel as a spirit rising out of the earth, as an old man covered with a robe. The old man addressed Saul, probably through the medium but in his own voice, and foretold Saul's doom.[35]

There is no suggestion in this story that it was merely imagination, and it is told in a matter-of-fact way. There were many mediums in the land, but Saul himself, and later reformers, tried to forbid their practices. The Hebrew prophets were strongly opposed to such seances, probably because they saw in them rivalry to the worship of God. So Isaiah said:

> When they say to you,
> Seek those that have familiar spirits,
> and the wizards that chirp and mutter,
> Should not a people seek their God?
> Should they consult the dead
> on behalf of the living?[36]

It is remarkable that the great scriptures of the world rarely describe mediums and seances, and their teachings about the soul and immortality are established from other arguments than

*We all have a sense of our self,
which seems to be more
than the body,
and it is hard to think
that this will die.*

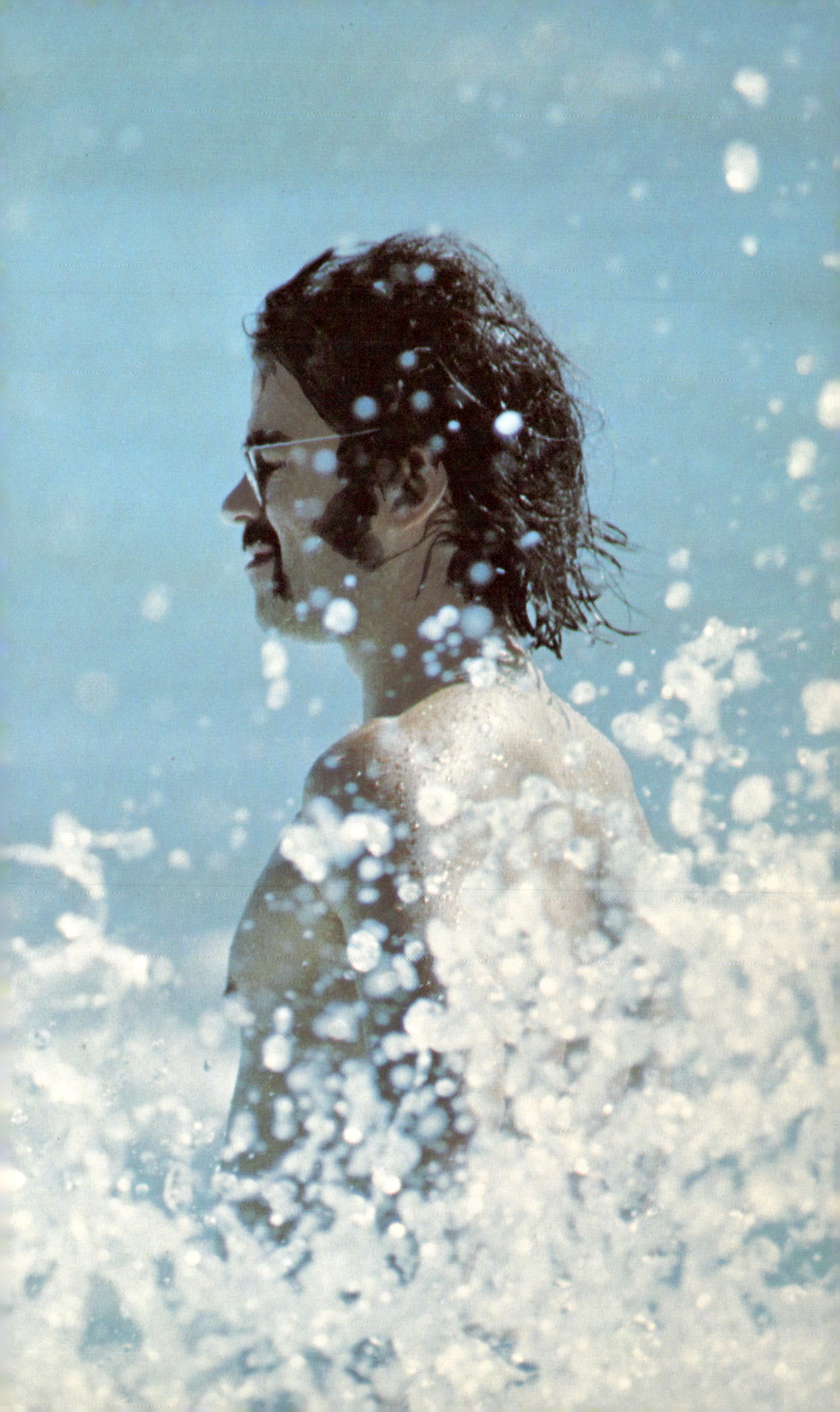

these. Even ordinary appearances or messages from the departed are rarely mentioned, with one great exception: the Resurrection appearances of Jesus.

Psychic research has gathered together a huge amount of literature on claims for seances and messages from the dead. Much of this has been rejected as confused, contradictory, or trivial. Messages which say that the weather is nice in the other world, or that we should do our part, or support our local sheriff, are insignificant or silly.

There is no doubt that some mediums honestly believe that they are in touch with departed spirits, and there have been famous mediums who appear to have had extraordinary powers which are not developed in normal people. However, there also are frauds, and this kind of practice very easily leads to deception. Claims to produce manifestations, such as "ectoplasms," substances which are supposed to come out of the body of the medium in trance, have often proved false. There is a very human tendency to try to strengthen the claims for mediums, by producing sights, making sounds, or inventing harmless messages.

Behind the proved frauds of some professional mediums and the doubts about others, there may remain enough evidence of abnormal statements or actions that is hard to explain away. Careful and eminent investigators have considered much of this evidence, and some are convinced that it ought to be taken more seriously than it has in the past.

C. D. Broad, a leading philosopher, discussing belief in the persistent existence of the soul, said:

> There are many quite well attested *paranormal* phenomena which strongly suggest such persistence, and a few which strongly suggest the full-blown survival of a human personality.[37]

He was not sure whether spiritualistic claims did prove survival of death or not, but he felt that such claims should not be dismissed without careful consideration. Another philosopher,

H. H. Price, is more positive and argues for existence after death both from psychic research and for general religious reasons. He thinks that some messages which are claimed to have come from the dead are limited by the difficulty of communication and the possibilities of distortion in the mind of the medium.

Establishing contact with the dead would be especially important for religion and for ordinary living. It would give us a much longer view of life and its value to know that existence does not end with the death of our bodies. On the other hand, we may not be told much about the quality of life after death. We should not ask where it is, since time and space will be very different or perhaps abolished. We should not ask where a spirit is, since location depends upon a body which can be measured, and we should not ask how long a spirit will remain in its present state. Life may continue in some way, but whether that is for a limited duration or everlasting is not so important as the kind of life it could be.

THE RESURRECTION
OF JESUS 9

Most founders and leaders of great religions have not been killed, though they have often been misunderstood and sometimes persecuted. The philosopher Socrates was condemned to drink poison, and the prophet Zoroaster was perhaps killed by rival priests. Jesus was murdered by the political scheming of Sadducee priests in league with Roman rulers. Other religious leaders are believed to have gone to Heaven or Nirvana after death, but of Jesus alone it is said that he rose again from the dead and appeared to his followers.

The Resurrection of Jesus has been central to Christian faith, but nowadays it is often neglected or placed so far away from ordinary experience as to be incomprehensible. Looking at a book on immortality by a Christian philosopher, I find that, while he argues about body and mind, reincarnation and the nature of Heaven, he has only one reference to the Resurrection of Jesus. This is on the next to last page and in a few lines which say that it must be understood in the light of the faith as a whole. Surely this is inadequate, because traditionally the Resurrection has been central to Christian belief about the soul and life after death.[38]

The Bible says that Jesus appeared to his disciples after death, and in some ways these appearances may have been like those which "psychic" or spiritualistic people describe for other apparitions. There has been a general dislike among modern Christian teachers of making any comparison of the appearances of Jesus with those of others, although if no comparisons are made, the subject can easily become unreal

46

and too far beyond our own experience. It is partly this remoteness of common teachings about the Resurrection that makes the subject so difficult for many people: it is outside the range of anything else that they have heard about or known.

It is clear that Jesus had "psychic" or "paranormal" powers. All four Gospels record miracles performed by him, and if these also are not to remain incomprehensible by having no connection with our own experience, many of them can be compared with psychiatric treatment in our own day. There are also many healers who would seem to have gifts comparable with those of Jesus. Blindness, paralysis, skin diseases, and other disorders can sometimes be cured by a combination of faith in the patient and skill in the healer. The Gospels often say, "May it be done according to your faith," but the forceful personality of Jesus himself would be a powerful stimulus to arouse such faith.

Other marvels, sometimes called "nature miracles," like stilling the storm (or the frightened disciples), walking on the water, or changing water into wine, are admittedly beyond our present understanding. They may be accepted literally, or criticized for contradictions, or interpreted as parables, or left until we have better knowledge of the "laws" of nature, but it is certain that the Gospel writers recorded these events because they believed they aroused and strengthened faith both in the first people who saw them and in later followers of the Christian way.

There are five places in the New Testament—in each of the four Gospels and in Paul's First Letter to the Corinthians—where accounts of the Resurrection of Jesus are found. All the Gospels contain several Resurrection stories. There are some apparent contradictions, but these may show that efforts were not made to force all the narratives into complete agreement.

Paul wrote before the Gospels were written, and in I Corinthians there is his brief summary. "Christ appeared to Cephas (Peter), then to the twelve, then to over five hundred brethren at once . . . then he appeared to James, then to all the apostles, and last of all he appeared to me." It is significant that Paul includes his own vision of Christ on an equal footing with the other appearances, and this must refer to his experience on the road to Damascus related in Acts 9. Here it is said that "a light shone round about Paul," that he heard the voice of Jesus, and that Jesus had appeared to him in the way."[39]

The appearances of Jesus summarized by Paul have some parallels in the Gospels. Luke says that Jesus "appeared to Simon (Peter)," apparently first, then to two disciples on the road, and to the rest in the upper room. John, rather later, gives two appearances in the upper room and then one appearance to Peter and other disciples when they had returned to their fishing in Galilee. He also adds an appearance to Mary Magdalene in the garden. Matthew gives an appearance to the woman on the way home and to the eleven disciples in Galilee. The end of Mark is known to have been cut short (at 16:8) and completed later.[40]

All the Gospels, but not Paul, refer to the grave of Jesus being found empty. In Mark and Luke a young man or angel was there to instruct the women to tell Peter and the rest that Jesus would see them in Galilee. Matthew adds details about sealing the tomb, the keepers and an earthquake, and John gives particulars of the folded clothes in the grave. Because the idea of the empty tomb is very difficult to understand (like "nature miracles"), some modern people either reject the resurrection altogether or push it away to the region of the incomprehensible and irrelevant. It may be that the stories originated in a mistake, in looking in the wrong place, but that would not explain visions of men in white or angels. It may have been a story that grew up gradually to account for the removal of the body of Jesus from the power of the Romans, but that raises more problems than it solves. Some writers, like Father Ward in his book *The Psychic Powers of Christ,* think that Jesus could dematerialize his body during life by vanishing from his questioners or walking on the sea, and so at death the process of dematerialization was hastened. The tomb was empty, the particles of the body of Jesus could be reassembled or dispersed, or his "astral" body could pass through stone walls.[41]

Man is only a reed,
the weakest thing in nature,
but he is a reed
that thinks.

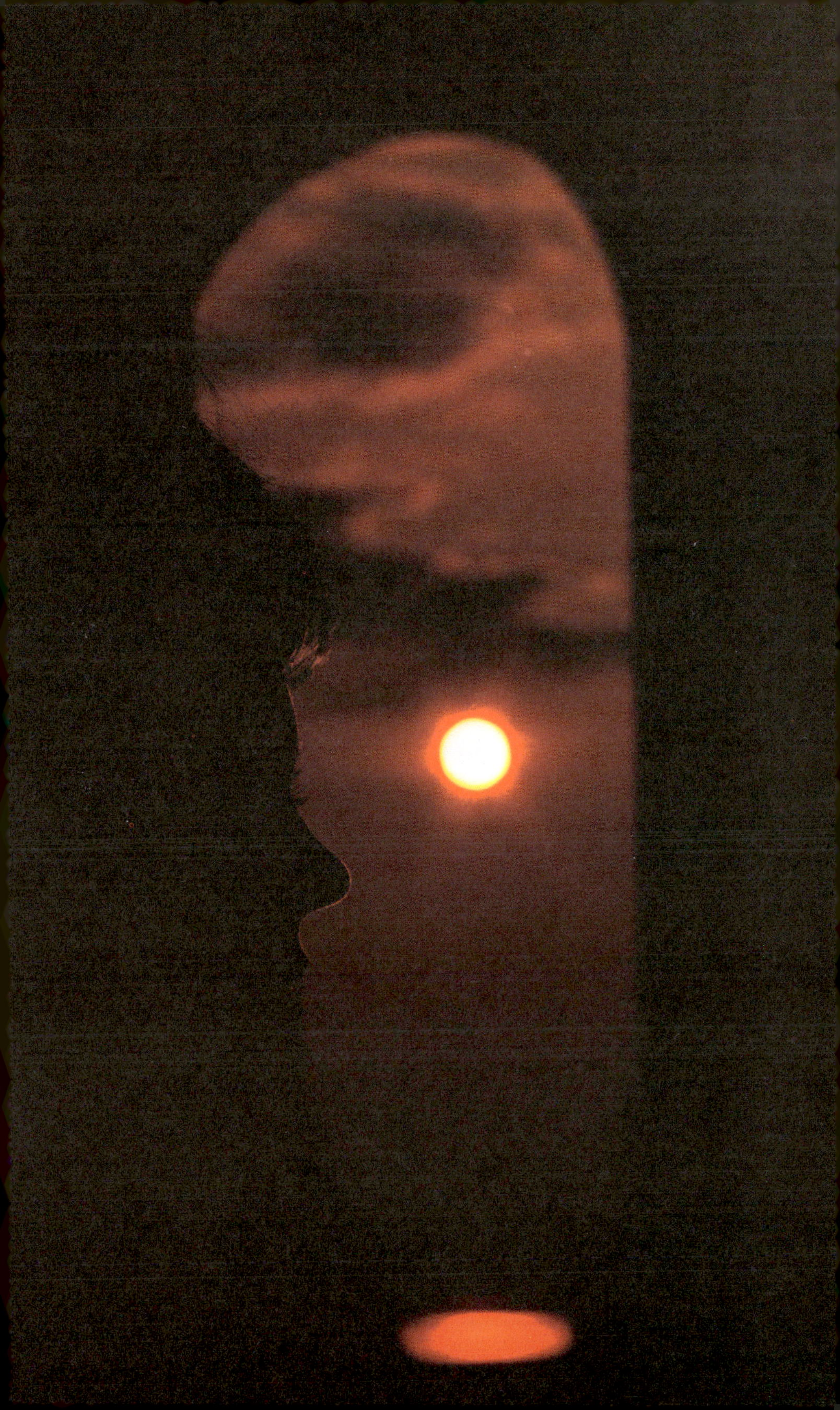

In several of the stories there is an air of strangeness. On the road to Emmaus the two disciples did not recognize Jesus until he sat at the table with them and broke the bread. Mary in the garden thought at first that Jesus was the gardener. When the eleven disciples saw him on a mountain in Galilee, some doubted until Jesus came nearer. John says that when the disciples saw Jesus by the lake, they did not recognize him until the beloved disciple said, "It is the Lord."

There is opposition in the Gospels to the notion that the disciples saw a ghost. Luke even says Jesus told them to touch his hands and feet and that he ate a piece of fish to prove that he was not a spirit. Clearly there was no spiritualistic seance, no medium or mumbo-jumbo, or table-rapping, or ectoplasm. The appearances of Jesus were occasional, occurring in different places and to several people, within the ranks of disciples and friends. It might be said that they were hallucinations, imagined by hysterical women, but there were collective as well as single experiences. Most of the disciples were men and included skeptics like the disciple Thomas.

What is clear, if the narratives are read without prejudice, is that they flow naturally from the earlier accounts of the life and Crucifixion of Jesus. They are stories of faith. They are not told in any way different from the rest of the Gospel. They all begin with the initiative of Jesus. It is he, according to all accounts, who appears; it was not the disciples who invented the visions or imagined that they were seeing things.

Jesus appeared to the disciples in their utter despair and lack of faith after his death to show them that death is not the end, that he had submitted himself completely to evil but that God had raised him up in victory. He came to them in the garden, on the road, in the room, at their work, so that they began to expect him at any time. At last they learned the lesson of his unseen presence, and his visible appearance was no longer necessary, except on special occasions such as to Paul. Then he ended his appearances with the assurance: "I am with you always, until the end of the world."[42]

SPIRITUAL BODY 10

Paul began his fifteenth chapter of I Corinthians with short references to the Resurrection appearances of Jesus, saying, "If in this life only we have hoped in Christ, we are of all men most miserable." Then he proceeded to consider the resurrection of all believers. It is a pity that many later discussions of the Resurrection of Jesus have isolated it from the death and the future of us all, for each of these help in understanding the other.

Paul tackles the question, How are the dead raised? He dismisses at once the notion that the same physical body can continue after death as it did on earth, for obviously this is impossible. He does not discuss dematerialization or levitation, but turns directly to a comparison from nature. A seed is sown in the ground and a blade of corn comes up. It is not the same body that rises up, yet the new one will not grow without the death of the old body. God gives a new form to the corn, so that life develops from life.

This is similarly true for the resurrection of the dead. The body is sown in corruption, but it is raised up incorruptible. "It is sown a natural body, it is raised a spiritual body." Paul compares the first body, or flesh which we receive from our parents with descent from a common ancestor, Adam, and he compares the spiritual body of life after death with the "life-giving spirit" that is in Christ. The Resurrection of Christ is the "first fruits," but all those who follow him will be made alive in and with him after death. Hence the Resurrection of Christ was in a spiritual body, and ours will be also.

Paul's teaching of a "spiritual body" is of great importance, but it has often been neglected or misunderstood. The Apostles'

Creed wrongly speaks of the "resurrection of the flesh," and this is usually nicely mistranslated in English as "resurrection of the body." This arose from a mistaken attempt to make heaven a fixed location. John's Gospel says that the grave clothes of Jesus were left in the tomb and that he then appeared to his followers. I once received a skeptical question as to whether Jesus appeared naked. I might have thought of Joan of Arc's retort, "Do you think that God cannot afford clothes for him?", but I preferred to attempt an explanation similar to Paul's of the resurrection of a spiritual body.

There have been many Christians in the past who have thought that the flesh and bones would be gathered together somehow at the Last Judgment, and they opposed the practice of cremation because that would make it difficult. Some doctors who find it hard to believe in life after death seem to be objecting chiefly to the notion of the resurrection of the flesh, but Paul positively asserts that the flesh is not raised up: a new body appears that is not the same as the earthly body since it is a new creation by God.

The idea of a spiritual body is useful because of the difficulty of imagining a "disembodied spirit" or a "pure spirit." If there is any continuing identity of ourselves after death or of any fellowship with other people, it might seem essential to have some kind of body. This might be like the body we have in dreams and would seem to give us a continuing identity. However, a body may not be necessary for identity, since awareness of ourselves, self-consciousness, might exist without embodiment. Paul is content to give no description of the spiritual body beyond saying that God gives it "as it pleases him."

Some dead persons may have personal identity for indefinite periods, and this may be an explanation of appearances and hauntings which continue for months, or even centuries. For others, transformation in the spiritual world may be more

*Certainly something
survives death,
for there is change
and re-creation.*

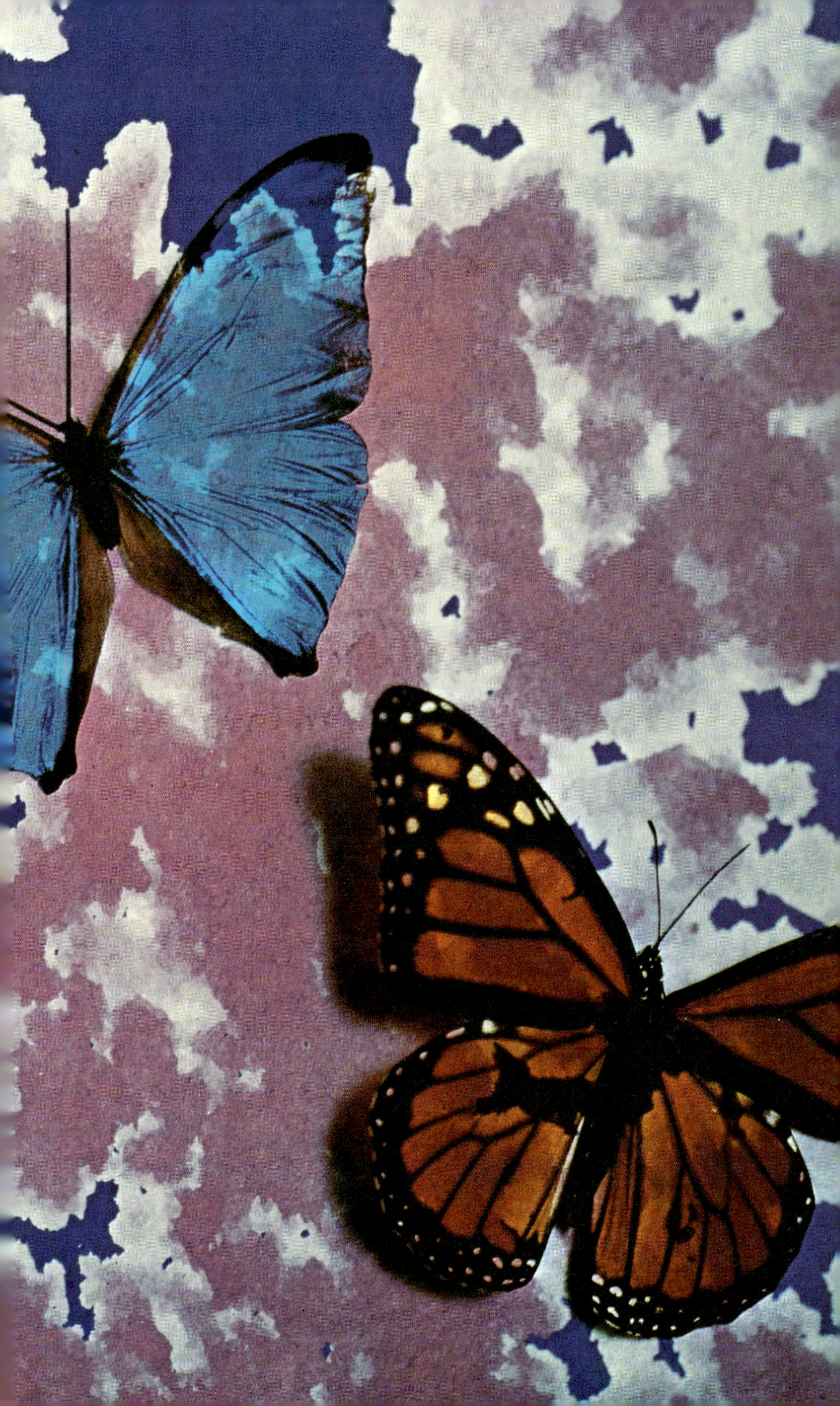

immediate and complete, though whether distinguishing characteristics remain which would enable individual recognition, or example in heaven, may be debated.

There are some teachers and religions that seem to think that at death all personality is lost, as a drop is lost in the ocean. The Indian Upanishads give this example:

> The eastern rivers flow towards the east
> and the western to the west.
> They go from sea to sea, and become the sea.
> When they are there they do not know that
> "I am this one," or "I am that one."
> Even so although all creatures here
> have come forth from Being,
> they do not know, "We have come out of Being." . . .
> That which is its finest essence,
> the whole world has that as its soul,
> That is Reality. That is the Soul. You are That.[43]

The rivers become part of the sea, and they do not know that they have emerged from Being. But man can know this; he is told that Being is the universal Soul and that he himself as soul is that universal Soul. For man there is a different kind of particularity to be overcome, and this is shown in another example.

> When a man is dying his voice goes into his mind,
> his mind into breath, his breath into heat,
> the heat into the highest divinity.[44]

Man loses particular details of his physical body in the life after death, and he becomes united with the supreme Soul. Unlike a river merging into the sea, he does not lose consciousness. On the contrary, man enlarges it and gains the supreme consciousness, the highest reality, which is the perfection and goal of the world beyond. Hence a popular name for the divine is Being-Consciousness-Bliss. That perfect Being, that fullest Consciousness, and that ultimate Bliss are the perfections of eternal life.

HEAVEN 11

Popular books have criticized traditional religious pictures of a "three-decker universe" with Heaven, Earth, and Hell and with God as an "old man in the sky."

The Lord's Prayer speaks of "Our Father which art in Heaven," but this phrase was used by Jews, who out of reverence did not want to utter the name of God directly, and so it means "God our Father," without implying that he is located in the sky. The imagery of heaven as the abode of God has long been recognized as picture language. Many writers down through the ages have said that the notion of heaven as a place in the clouds, where God is sitting on a throne, is like an illustration in a child's picture book. The sky is a useful symbol of God, who is above and greater than men.

That we go to heaven when we die and live there "above the bright blue sky," sitting on clouds or playing harps, is hardly acceptable in these days of space exploration, even if men have only penetrated a tiny corner of a solar system. Much of Christian thought has been influenced by the last book in the New Testament, the Book of Revelation, which gives vivid pictures of God on a throne in front of a sea of glass surrounded by angels and countless other beings. There comes a great war in heaven, with demons being cast down into a bottomless pit; finally a new heaven and earth with rivers and trees and perpetual light appear. Such descriptions of heaven and hell, reinforced by details from eastern and especially Persian, sources, provided symbols for paintings and stained glass windows in churches in the Middle Ages.

It is not only Christians who have used visual symbols of life after death but other religions also; for example, the Moslem paradise is very much the same as the heaven of Christianity. In India, the Upanishads speak of the dead rising up to the sun and moon, arriving at the world of the gods where there are beautiful sights and sounds. All these are symbolic: there is an "ageless" river, and "extensive" hall, and a couch of "unmeasured splendor." The soul crosses the river "with his mind alone," and when God questions him, saying, "Who are you?", he replies, "I am what you are, the Real."[45]

Buddhism also, like practically all religions, has had many pictures of heaven. The Buddha lived in the "heaven of delight" before his last birth on earth, and he was accompanied by thousands of angelic beings. In northern (Mahayana) Buddhism, in China, Tibet, Korea, and Japan, there are many stories of Buddhas who live in Western paradises or Buddha-fields. There is a Pure Land beyond earth, which is the kind of idealized mountain retreat like that which was imagined by James Hilton for the Shangri La of his *Lost Horizon*.

Pictures of heaven are necessary for our imagination, but exaggerations need correction, and the Buddhists tackled this in discussions about Nirvana. Nirvana means literally "blown out," like turning off a lamp. Human desires similarly must be extinguished. At death the perfect man has blown out his passions and attains Nirvana. In Europe the word Nirvana has sometimes been defined as "extinction," yet it does not mean that the soul is extinct—only our cravings and desires are eliminated. Its nature is indicated by similes in Buddhist writings.

> Nirvana is lofty like a mountain peak,
> Nirvana is immovable like a mountain peak,
> Nirvana is free from desires like a mountain peak . . . .
> No defilements can grow in Nirvana
> as no seeds can grow on a mountain peak.[46]

*The sky
is a useful symbol of God,
who is above
and greater than men.*

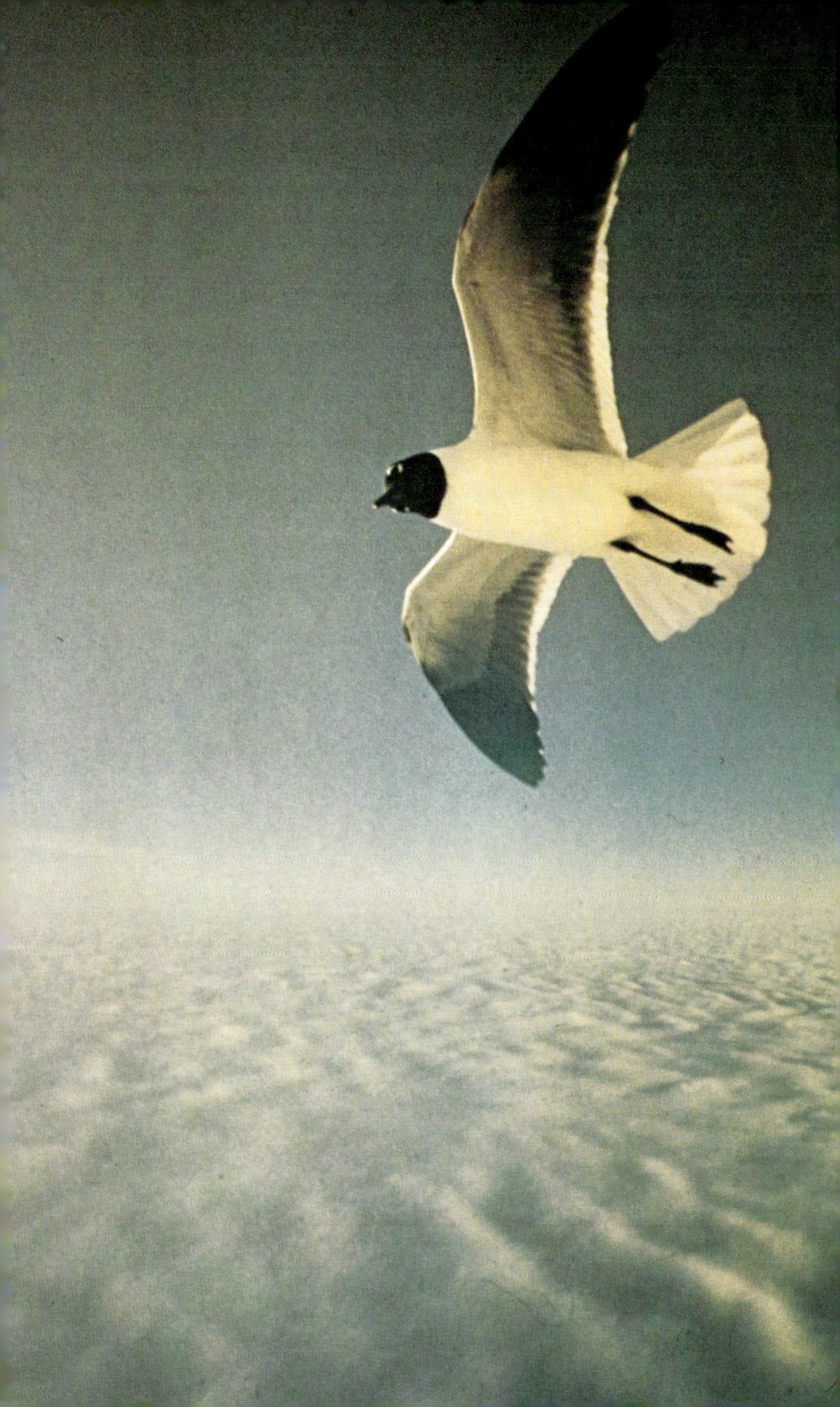

The condition of beings who have attained Nirvana is difficult to describe if symbols are not used. Even of the Buddha himself, can it be said that he is here or there? In fact language, even negative, is inadequate.

> Since Buddha, even when actually present on earth,
> is incomprehensible,
> it is foolish to say of him . . .
> that after dying the Buddha is, or is not,
> or both is and is not,
> or neither is nor is not.[47]

In Christian teaching also, the imagery used about heaven is picture language, but the final truth is indescribable. After the Book of Revelation one of the most influential writings has been *The Divine Comedy*, by the fourteenth-century Italian poet Dante. Here in the three worlds of hell, purgatory and paradise, Dante describes in lurid detail many sufferings and joys in the hereafter, with names and particulars of famous figures of history and people of his time. At the very end of this long poem Dante sees the vision of the indescribable God, the Beatific Vision which is the goal of Christian saints.

> I gazed upon that eternal Light so long
> that my eyes were wearied.
> In its depths I was the scattered leaves
> of all the universe,
> bound by Love into one volume . . .
> and as I gazed I was filled with wonder . . . .
> My desire and will were moved,
> like a wheel moving smoothly,
> by the Love that moves the sun
> and all the other stars.[48]

As I gazed
I was filled with wonder.

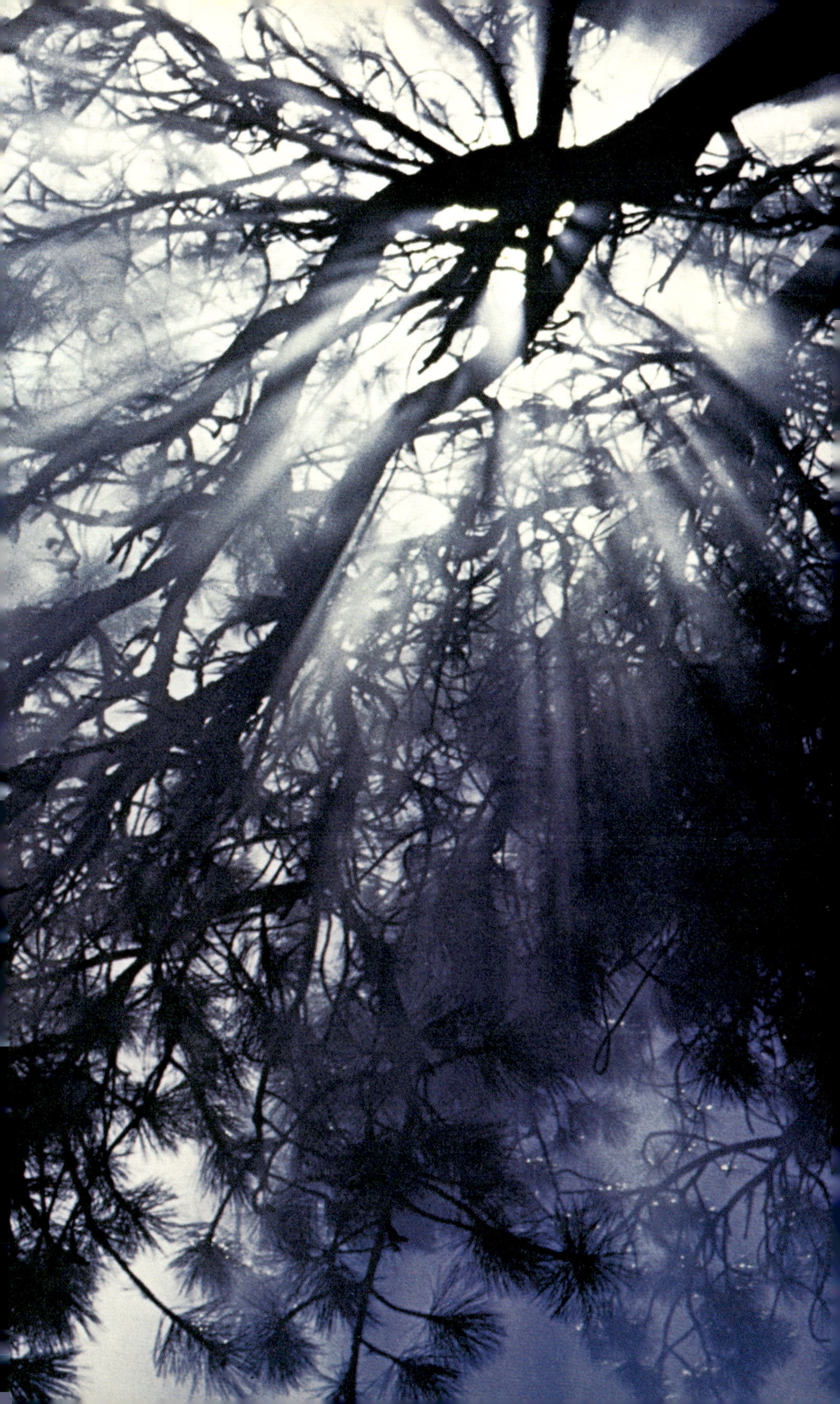

Heaven has been described in many ways, and so have hell and purgatory. The notions of one hell or many hells are found in both Eastern and Western religions, and Hindu and Buddhist popular tales speak of frightful places where demons torture the damned. The Bhagavad Gita talks in a more lofty tone, but it says that cruel and hateful people will constantly be thrown back into the ceaseless round of rebirth and that they will sink down to the lowest path without ever attaining God.[49] At the end of a world cycle they would all be dissolved, though purified men of faith might escape from the round of re-incarnation.

The notion of hell probably came into Christianity from Persia, since it is hardly found in the Old Testament where the dead are thought to be like shadows under the ground.[50] The Gospel, like the Gita, speaks of "eternal" punishment, but this is not "everlasting" in the old sense of going on forever. Eternal means age-long during the present world cycle, and everlasting life as mere endlessness is inferior to the quality of eternal life in the knowledge of God.

The idea of purgatory arose fairly early in the Christian era as a modification of the stark contrast between heaven and hell. It was thought that those who still had sins, or their results, to bear would suffer in purgatory and be "purged" before the final Judgment and the Vision of God. Prayers for the dead had probably been practiced long before this, since they are found in many religions and are recorded on early Christian grave inscriptions, but they would be strengthened by the belief that such prayers could help souls in purgatory. At the Reformation, indulgences, offered by the Church for the pains of purgatory, were rejected. It was taught that the righteous are freed from all sin and go straight to heaven. However, forms of belief rather like purgatory have been held by some Protestants, especially if they believe in the progress of souls after death.

Belief in Universalism, that all men will finally be saved and that hell is not everlasting, was held by some Christian teachers in the past and has grown in the last two centuries. Moslem mystics also thought that all souls would be saved, even the worst. Even the Devil himself, who according to Moslem belief had refused God's command to bow down to Adam, would be saved. He was really the truest worshipper since God alone should be worshipped, so Universalists believe that God is love and wills all men to know him and that his purpose must be fulfilled. The greatest obstacle, it is often argued, is human free will and whether some men are so perverse that they will always resist the love of God, or whether their evil is caused by ignorance which will pass away.

THE GOALS OF LIFE 12

"Pie in the sky when you die" used to be a criticism of religion. Either there is pie in heaven or there is not, but pie on earth is also important. If too much attention is given to the problems of life after death, there is a danger that it will be regarded as the most important life, while our existence on earth is looked upon as miserable and unnecessary. For many people life here is unhappy, but for many others it is not, and the aim should be to improve living conditions for everybody rather than to tell them that it does not matter because everything will be put right in heaven.

Part of the modern confusion about life after death is a natural reaction against the morbid attitudes to life and death which were expressed in past ages. In Victorian England hymns were sung which claimed that "I'm but a stranger here, heaven is my home."

Not only some kinds of Christianity, but Hindu and Buddhist religions in particular have been called "world-denying," because they valued renunciation of the world and living an austere life alone in the forest until death came. We are used to pictures of Indian holy men who lie on beds of nails, or hold up one arm till it withers away, or go blind gazing at the sun. But a

The aim should be to improve living conditions for everyone rather than to tell them it does not matter because everything will be put right in heaven.

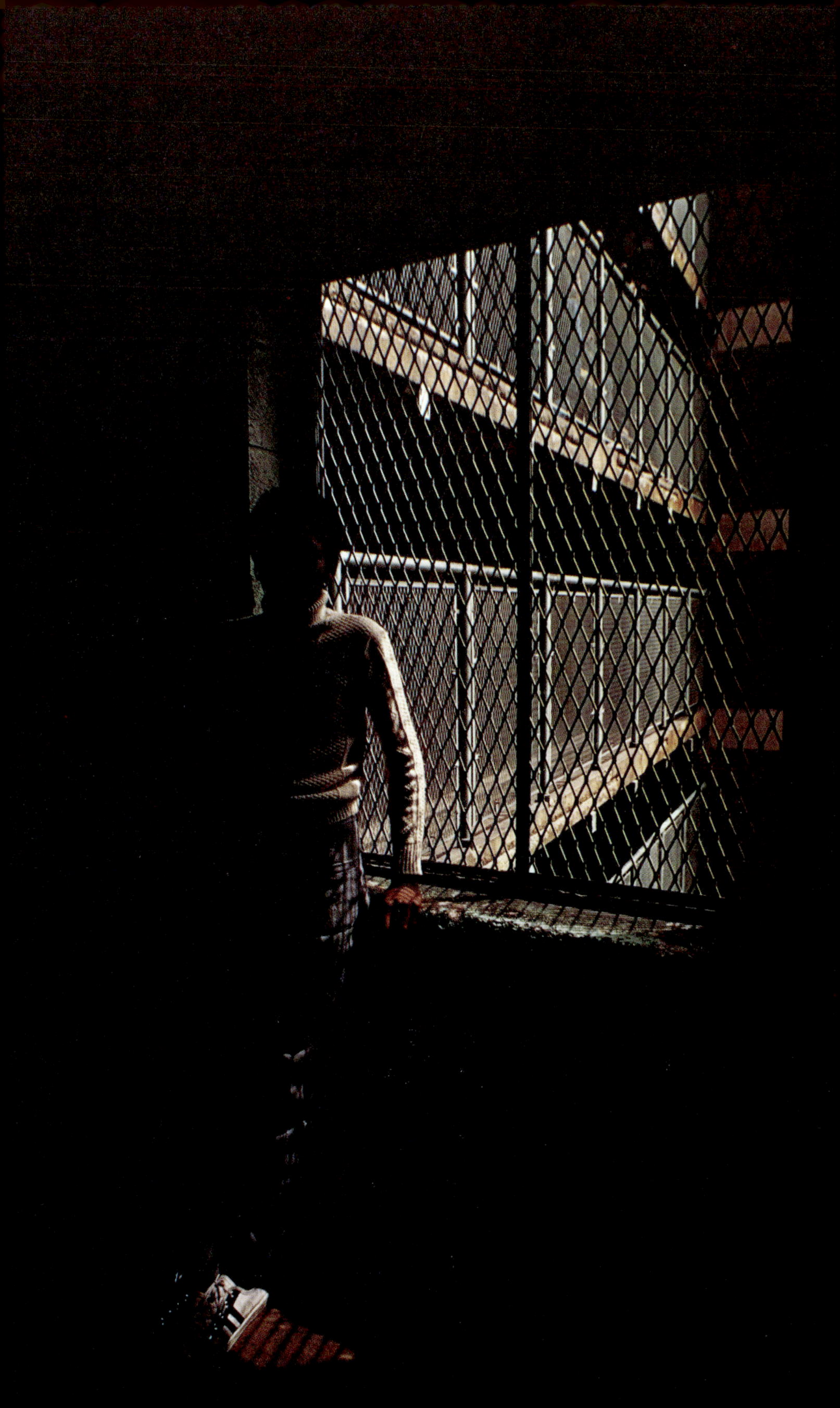

less extreme ideal was that of the man who would leave the world, find a lonely spot by a river and under a tree, and there meditate in solitude, though he would ensure that there was "a village nearby for support."

The religion of most people kept them fully in the world. The life of the normal Indian man was divided into four stages. First he was a student, then a householder, then a father and a grandfather. Only when he had seen his children's children, would he think of spending his last years in preparing for death by meditation. In other countries people retire to play golf, dig the garden or watch TV. India has had many great cultures, and the countless buildings, sculptures, paintings, poems, prose, medical and scientific achievements, show how their culture was really "world-affirming." Special holy men and philosophers may have abandoned the world, but the religion of ordinary people kept them close to the material as well as the spiritual needs of life.

Christianity has been called "world-affirming," and nowadays it lays great stress upon social, medical, and scientific work, but in the past it has also been "world-denying," with monasteries and celibate priests. There is probably a need for both world affirmation and world denial in great religious and cultural traditions. Material things are not enough. Man does not live by bread alone as the condition necessary for the good life.

Both spiritual and humanitarian reasons lie behind modern debates on pressing moral problems, such as euthanasia, contraception, abortion, capital punishment, suicide, and even heart transplants and possible brain transplants. There is uncertainty about life after death, a feeling that man deserves a full span of life and should not die "before his time" and a widespread conviction of the sacredness of life. There are dangers that a totalitarian state, or simply a bureaucratic one, might consider the lives of the old and sick as disposable. In discussions of abortion there is the question of at what point an embryo becomes a "living soul," whether at conception, gestation, or birth. Whether one believes in reincarnation or creation of a new soul does not make much difference here. Certainly belief in an immortal soul supports the sacredness of life, both of the mother and of her unborn child.

We have asked, Is death the end? and now we reply, No, by faith in resurrection or reincarnation. In both beliefs the quality of the future life is thought to be affected by the kind of life we live on earth. Does this mean that a man will not live a good life now if he does not believe in survival after death? Not necessarily; men may have many ideals. A man may work for the good of his family, for the state, for the poor, or for himself, but the quality of his ideal is likely to be more permanent and universal if he believes in an eternal and universal being, a divine mind or God. To act "as in the light of eternity" means that our actions are not just limited to a moment or a locality but that they should be done in such a way that we would want them always done like that.

Our behavior is deeply affected by our belief in the best kind of life, both now and after death. The psychologist Jung, from many years of experience, said that it was of great importance to believe in life after death so that meaning and purpose will be given to action.

> For most people it means a great deal to assume that their lives will have an indefinite continuity beyond their present existence. They live more sensibly, feel better, and are more at peace. . . . In the majority of cases the question of immortality is so urgent, so immediate, and also so ineradicable that we must make an effort to form some sort of view about it.[51]

What we call conscience is our true self responding to the eternal Being. This inmost self urges us to a perfection of life and actions, but perfection is hard to reach on earth. Thus, men have become convinced that there must be an eternal life, and endless progress. It is God who inspires our conscience and also gives us eternal life.

Yet we do live on earth, and our work must be to follow the old and plain commandments, to love God and our neighbors as ourselves. To concentrate efforts on ourselves, or on our own souls, leads to self-destruction, but to forget ourselves in a higher cause if to find our true selves, now and eternally.

> Whoever seeks to gain his life will lose it,
> but whoever loses his life will save it.[52]

References

1. Job 14:13
2. W. Shakespeare, *Hamlet* III i
3. Apology 40-1
4. Plato, *Phaedo* 118
5. Job 14: 7-10
6. T. Carlyle, *Sartor Resartus* 3
7. Svetāsvatara Upanishad 3, 18
8. Samyutta Nikāya 3, 19f
9. R. Wilhelm, *The Secret of the Golden Flower*, 1965 ed. p.22.
10. Pascal, *Pensées* 6, 347
11. Luke 12: 4
12. Svetāsvatara Upanishad 1 and 6
13. Chāndogya Upanishad 6, 2
14. Tao Tê Ching 25 and 42
15. Chāndogya Upanishad 3, 14:3-4
16. Genesis 2:7
17. Ecclesiastes 12:7
18. Bhagavad Gītā 12, 6-7
19. Romans 8:38-39
20. John 17:3
21. John 3:16
22. Bhagavad Gītā 2, 20
23. W. Wordsworth, *Intimations of Immortality* 5
24. Plato, *Phaedo* 70, 76
25. Plato, *Republic* 10, 614f
26. Chāndogya Upanishad 5, 3, 2
27. Brihad-āranyaka Upanishad 4, 4, 5
28. Bhagavad Gītā 2, 22
29. *ibid.* 2, 18 and 20
30. Vinaya Pitaka 3, 3-6
31. G.B. Shaw, *Saint Joan*, 1
32. From the hymn "O God our help in ages past"
33. F.L.K. Hsu, *Under the Ancestor's Shadow*, p. 52
34. Hebrews 12:1
35. 1 Samuel 28:7ff
36. Isaiah 8:19
37. C.D. Broad, *Lectures on Psychical Research*, p. 430

38. H.D. Lewis, *The Self and Immortality*, p. 208
39. 1 Corinthians 15:3-8; Acts 9:3-17
40. Luke 24:34; John 20:14-29; Matthew 28:9f; Mark 16:8
41. J.S.M. Ward, *The Psychic Powers of Christ*, p. 77ff
42. Matthew 28:20
43. Chāndogya Upanishad 6, 10
44. *ibid*, 6, 8, 6-7
45. Kaushītaki Upanishad 1, 2-6
46. Milinda's Questions 322
47. Samyutta Nikāya 3, 118
48. Dante, *Divine Comedy*, Paradisco, 33, 82ff, 142ff
49. Bhagavad Gītā 16, 19-20
50. Psalm 88:10ff
51. C.G. Jung, *Memories, Dreams, Reflections*
52. Luke 17:33